SENSES

HEARING

Anita Ganeri

W
FRANKLIN WATTS
LONDON•SYDNEY

 An Appleseed Editions book

First published in 2014 by Franklin Watts
338 Euston Road, London NW1 3BH

© 2012 Appleseed Editions

Created by Appleseed Editions Ltd,
Well House, Friars Hill, Guestling,
East Sussex TN35 4ET

Designed and illustrated by Guy Callaby
Edited by Mary-Jane Wilkins

A CIP record for this book is available from
the British Library

ISBN 978 1 4451 3152 8

Dewey Classification: 612.8'5

Picture acknowledgements
l = left, r = right, c = centre, t = top, b = bottom
page 1 iStockphoto/Thinkstock; 2 Digital Vision/Thinkstock,
3t Sergey Fedenko/Shutterstock, 3c Gorilla/Shutterstock,
3b Gelpi/Shutterstock; 4 Jupiterimages/Thinkstock; 6 Hemer
a/Thinkstock; 7 ingret/Shutterstock; 8c IrinaK/Shutterstock,
b iStockphoto/Thinkstock; 9 ravl/Shutterstock; 10 Zoonar/
Thinkstock; 11 iStockphoto/Thinkstock; 13 iStockphoto/
Thinkstock; 14 iStockphoto/Thinkstock; 15 Stockbyte/
Thinkstock; 16 Ilike/Shutterstock; 17 iStockphoto/Thinkstock;
18 Sportlibrary/Shutterstock; 19 Jupiterimages/Thinkstock;
20 auremar/Shutterstock; 21 andras_csontos/Shutterstock;
22c iStockphoto/Thinkstock, b Johan Swanepoel/
Shutterstock; 23 borkiss/Shutterstock; image beneath
folios Jupiterimages/Thinkstock
Cover: Thinkstock

Printed in China

Franklin Watts is a division of Hachette Children's Books,
an Hachette UK company
www.hachette.co.uk

Contents

Hear, hear

What happens when you listen to music? What sounds can you hear?

You use your ears to listen to someone playing the guitar.

Hearing is one of your senses. Your senses tell you about the world around you.

Your five senses are:

sight

hearing

touch

taste

smell

You see with your eyes

You hear with your ears

You touch with your fingers

You taste with your tongue

You smell with your nose

What can you hear?

There are lots of different sounds. Some sounds are **loud**, such as a jet plane taking off.

Some sounds are **soft**, such as a cat purring or a person whispering.

What are sounds?

Sounds make the air wobble. High sounds make the air wobble very quickly.

A mouse makes a high sound when it squeaks.

Dogs can pick up sounds that are too high for you to hear.

Low sounds

make the air wobble slowly.

How do you hear?

You hear sounds with your two ears. Your earflaps catch the sounds.

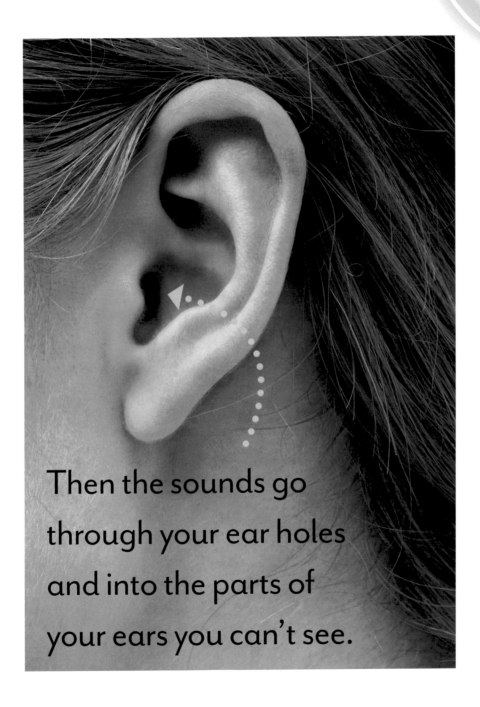

Then the sounds go through your ear holes and into the parts of your ears you can't see.

Inside your ears

The sounds go down a tube to some thin skin, called your ear drum. They make it wobble.

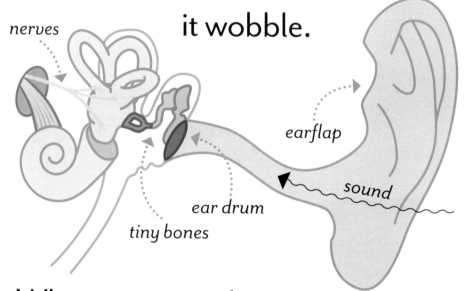

nerves

earflap

ear drum

tiny bones

sound

When your ear drum wobbles, it makes three tiny ear bones wobble, too.

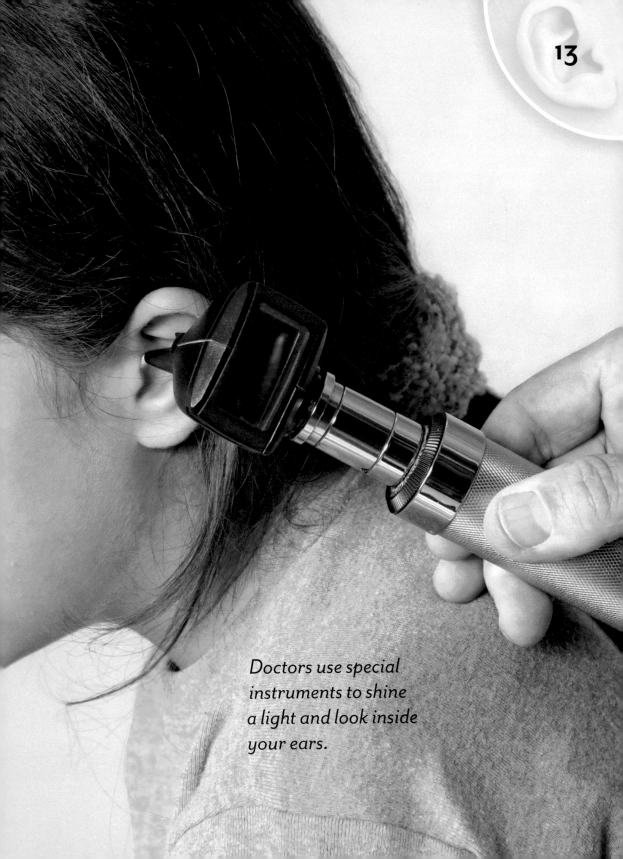

Doctors use special instruments to shine a light and look inside your ears.

Hearing messages

The wobbling goes deeper inside your ears where there is liquid and hairy nerves.

The hairs deep inside your ears are a bit like the bristles on a toothbrush.

The liquid wobbles and pulls on the hairs. The hairs send **messages** to your brain to tell you what you can hear.

Your brain tells you what the person on the phone is saying to you.

Two ears

Why do you have two ears?
It helps to tell you where sounds
are coming from.

Sounds hit one ear before
the other, so the wobbles are
stronger in the first ear.

Two ears help you to hear sounds all around you.

In a spin

Apart from hearing, your ears also help you to balance and to spin round quickly.

Nerves send messages to your brain. Your brain tells your body what to do so that you don't fall over.

If you spin round then stop, you feel dizzy. This is because the liquid inside your ears keeps swirling about.

Being deaf

Some people cannot hear very well. People who can't hear are deaf.

Loud sounds can hurt your ears and stop them working properly.

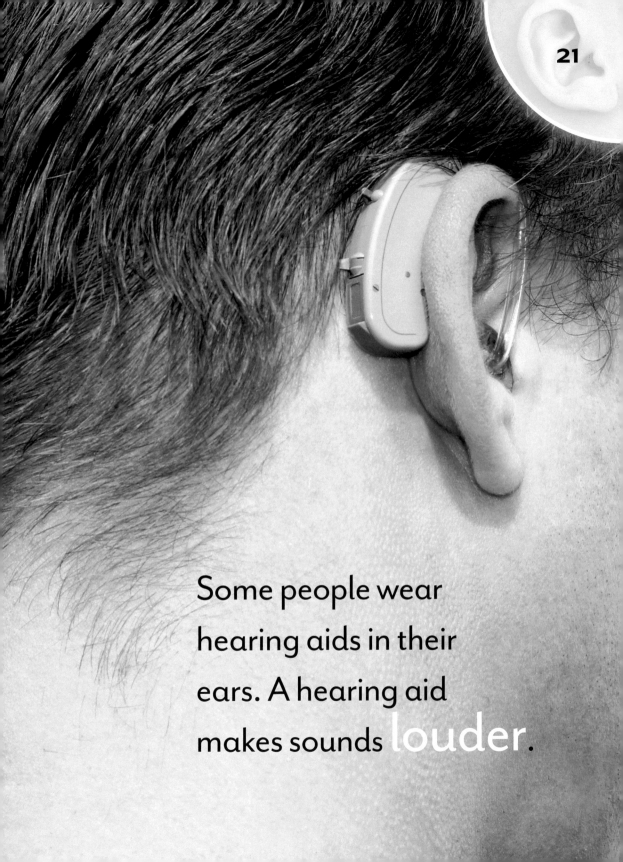

Some people wear hearing aids in their ears. A hearing aid makes sounds louder.

Hearing facts

The tiny bones in your ears are the smallest bones in your body. They are about the same size as grains of rice.

This shows just how small your ear bones are!

African elephants have the biggest ears of any animal. Their earflaps are as big as a single bed sheet.

You have yellowish wax inside your ears to catch tiny specks of dirt and dust.

Some animals, such as rabbits and cats, can move their ears to help them catch sounds.

Useful words

ear drum
A thin piece of skin that stretches across the tube inside your ear.

earflaps
The parts of your ears you can see on the outside of your head.

nerves
Thin, long wires inside your body that carry messages between your body and brain.

sounds
Another word for the noises you can hear.

Index